A Farm

by Meg Dandino
illustrated by Gary Undercuffler

Pre-Decodable 3

I0806551

Mc Graw Hill Education

Bothell, WA • Chicago, IL • Columbus, OH • New York, NY

MHEonline.com

Copyright © 2015 McGraw-Hill Education

All rights reserved. No part of this publication may be reproduced or distributed in any form or by any means, or stored in a database or retrieval system, without the prior written consent of McGraw-Hill Education, including, but not limited to, network storage or transmission, or broadcast for distance learning.

Send all inquiries to:
McGraw-Hill Education
8787 Orion Place
Columbus, OH 43240

ISBN: 978-0-02-145668-0
MHID: 0-02-145668-2

Printed in China

9 10 11 12 13 DSS 28 27 26 25 24

a 

pig

a 

cow

a 

horse

a 

duck

a 

lamb

a 

farm